THE
BROADWAY
Trivia
GAME BOOK

By Jenine Zimmers

Copyright ©2022

What you need

- This book!
- 2+ players
- A smartphone timer or stopwatch
- Scoring method (Pen and paper, or smartphone)

How to play

Choose a person to keep score.

Break into two teams. Team 1 reads the first question for Team 2. If the team answers correctly, they earn the number of points for that question. (Basic trivia questions are worth 1, 2 or 3 points based on difficulty. Correct answers are always found on the page that follows each question.) Then Team 1 passes the book to Team 2, who reads the next question. Continue passing the book back and forth and alternating questions.

If a team lands on a bonus round page, they will have an opportunity to earn up to 12 points. Some of these challenges involve a time limit. Read all instructions aloud when landing on a bonus round page, and use a timer when necessary. The question reader should keep track of correct answers in a bonus round, and tally the points for the scorekeeper.

Many of the challenges encourage you to sing — give your best Broadway performance! (Note: singing is always optional for players with stage fright.)

The team with the most points at the end wins. You may choose to play the entire book. For a shorter round, elect to end the game on page 50 or page 100, and pick up from there next time.

2 POINTS

Question

What was the last Broadway musical that Richard Rodgers and Oscar Hammerstein created, which debuted in 1959?

Answer

The Sound of Music

2 POINTS

Question

A helicopter was an unforgettable part of what musical that opened in 1991?

Answer

Miss Saigon

3 POINTS

Question

In what show did Kristin Chenoweth make her Broadway debut?

Answer

Steel Pier

3
POINTS

Question

What was the original title of
the musical *Oklahoma*?

Answer

Away We Go

BONUS
Round!

(Consider this a vocal warm-up!)

BONUS Round!

UP TO

6
POINTS

One at a time, read aloud each show and song title
without saying the missing word.
Players on the opposing team must fill in the missing word.
You are encouraged to sing your answers! No extra points
for singing ... but no points lost for off-key voices, either.
(1 point for each correct answer for a maximum of 6 points.)

1 *Bye Bye Birdie:* "How _____ to Be a Woman"
Answer: Lovely

2 *Avenue Q:* "I Wish I Could Go Back To _____"
Answer: College

3 *Gypsy:* "If Momma Was _____"
Answer: Married

4 *The Phantom of the Opera:* "Poor Fool, He Makes Me _____"
Answer: Laugh

5 *The Book of Mormon:* "All-American _____"
Answer: Prophet

6 *Mamma Mia:* "Thank You for the _____"
Answer: Music

2
POINTS

Question

In what city did
Les Misérables premiere?

Answer

Paris

2

POINTS

Question

What titular Broadway character is the "demon barber"?

Answer

Sweeney Todd

BONUS
Round!

(Still getting those pipes warm!)

BONUS Round!

UP TO

6
POINTS

One at a time, read aloud each show and song title
without saying the missing word.
Players on the opposing team must fill in the missing word.
You are encouraged to sing your answers! No extra points
for singing ... but no points lost for off-key voices, either.
(1 point for each correct answer for a maximum of 6 points.)

1 *Hamilton:* "The _____ Where It Happens"
Answer: Room

2 *Kinky Boots:* "Sex is in the _____"
Answer: Heel

3 *The Drowsy Chaperone:* "Toledo _____"
Answer: Surprise

4 *Sweet Charity:* "I'm the _____ Individual"
Answer: Bravest

5 *Carousel:* "A Real _____ Clambake"
Answer: Nice

6 *Pippin:* "No _____ at All"
Answer: Time

Question

In what year did the TKTS
discount booth debut
in Times Square?

Answer

1973

3
POINTS

Question

In what year did
the first theater open
on Broadway?

Answer

1735

Question

What number birthday does Bobbie celebrate in *Company*?

Answer

35th

2
POINTS

Question

In *La Cage Aux Folles*, what was La Cage Aux Folles?

Answer

A nightclub

POINTS

Question

In *The King and I*, the King is the ruler of where?

Answer

Siam

Question

In what country was
A Little Night Music set?

Answer

Sweden

BONUS
Round!

(Get ready for your grand entrance.)

BONUS Round!

UP TO

6
POINTS

It's all about those Broadway numbers! In the song title, that is. Read aloud each number and show title below. Opposing team players must name the song title from that show that contains that specific number. True Broadway fans will sing their answers! (1 point for each correct answer for a maximum of 6 points.)

1. Two, *Cabaret*
   Answer: "Two Ladies"

2. Ten, *A Chorus Line*
   Answer: "Dance: Ten; Looks: Three"

3. Six, *The 25th Annual Putnam County Spelling Bee*
   Answer: "I Speak Six Languages"

4. Five, *Little Women*
   Answer: "Five Forever"

5. Two, *Oliver!*
   Answer: "You've Got To Pick A Pocket Or Two"

6. Seven, *Camelot*
   Answer: "The Seven Deadly Virtues"

2 POINTS

Question

As of 2022, what is the highest-grossing musical of all time?

Answer

The Lion King
(more than $1.6 billion)

2
POINTS

Question

As of 2022, what musical has the greatest number of Tony Award nominations?

Answer

Hamilton (16)

BONUS
Round!

(Don't wait in the wings for this one.)

BONUS Round!

UP TO
6
POINTS

More Broadway numbers! Read aloud each number and show title below. Opposing team players must name the song title from that show that contains that specific number.
Die-hard fans will sing their answers!
(1 point for each correct answer for a maximum of 6 points.)

1   Nine, *42nd Street*
Answer: "About a Quarter to Nine"

2   Twelve, *A Chorus Line*
Answer: "Hello Twelve, Hello Thirteen, Hello Love"

3   Seventeen, *The Sound of Music*
Answer: "Sixteen Going on Seventeen"

4   One Hundred, *Wonderful Town*
Answer: "One Hundred Easy Ways"

5   Two, *Into the Woods*
Answer: "It Takes Two"

6   One, *The Three Musketeers*
Answer: "All For One"

Question

In what show did Idina Menzel
make her Broadway debut?

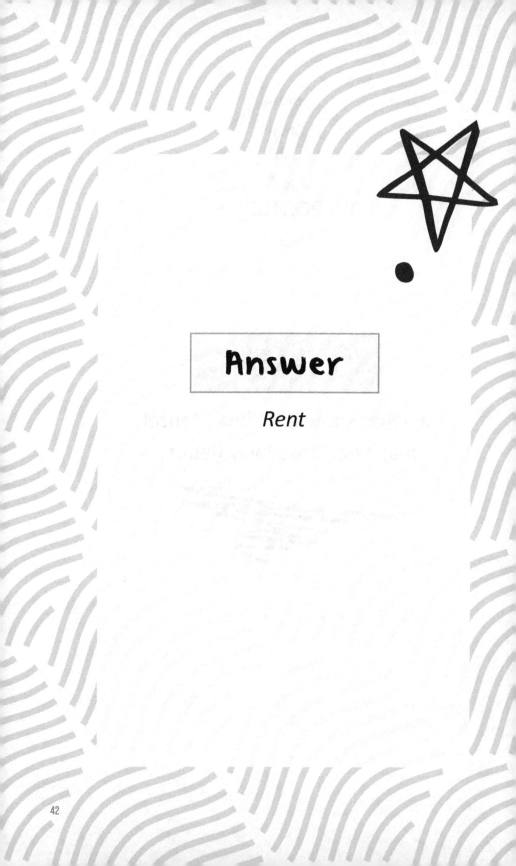

Answer

Rent

2

POINTS

Question

Which Broadway musical is based on Puccini's opera *Madame Butterfly*?

Answer

Miss Saigon

2
POINTS

Question

What musical featured the song "I'm Gonna Wash That Man Right Out of My Hair"?

Answer

South Pacific

2 POINTS

Question

The first song in the original production of *Cabaret* starts with what word?

Answer

Wilkommen

Question

What is the name of the carnivorous Venus flytrap plant in *Little Shop of Horrors*?

Answer

Audrey II

2 POINTS

Question

Annie Get Your Gun was
based on the real life
of whom?

Answer

Annie Oakley

3
POINTS

Question

Who were the first male and female actors to win a Tony Award for playing the same role on Broadway?

Answer

Ben Vereen and
Patina Miller, for their
performances as The
Leading Player (*Pippin*).

3
POINTS

Question

What was the first musical
ever on Broadway?

Answer

The Black Crook (1866)

BONUS
Round!

(No small parts, only small players.)

BONUS Round!

UP TO

4
POINTS

Only four Broadway theaters actually sit on the street Broadway.
Name them. You get four guesses total.
(1 point for each correct answer for a maximum of 4 points.)

The Winter Garden

The Roundabout

The Marquis

The Broadway Theatre

2

POINTS

Question

What nickname was given to the street Broadway because it was one of first in New York to be fully illuminated by electric bulbs in the 1890s?

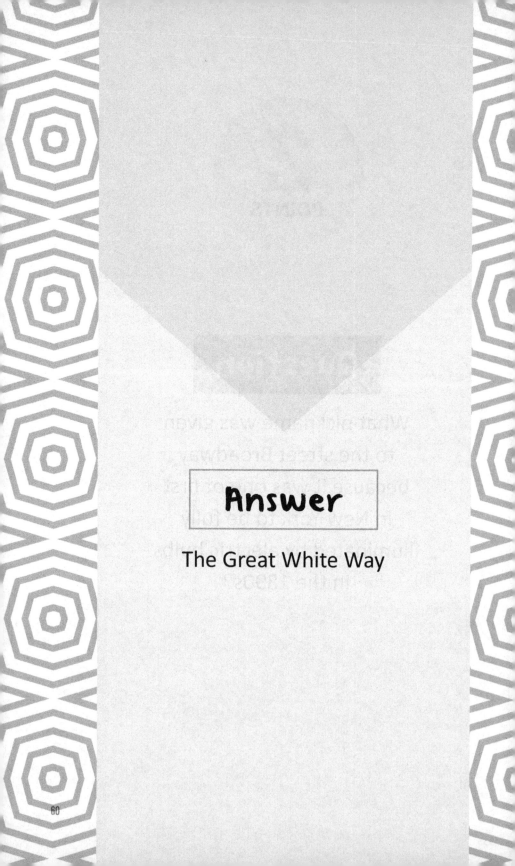

Answer

The Great White Way

2 POINTS

Question

As of 2022, what is the longest running show on Broadway?

Answer

The Phantom of the Opera

BONUS
Round!

(Break a leg!)

BONUS Round!

UP TO

4

POINTS

The Phantom of the Opera has the most performances on Broadway with more than 12,000. What four other shows round out the top five of all time through 2022?
You get four guesses total.
(1 point for each correct answer for a maximum of 4 points.)

Chicago

The Lion King

Cats

Les Misérables

1
POINT

Question

True or false: Broadway is the longest street in New York City.

Answer

True! It runs for 33 miles.

1

POINT

Question

True or false: Judy Garland
is said to frequently haunt
the Palace Theater?

Answer

True! She performed in the theater in the 1950s, and many have claimed to see her ghost near the door in the orchestra pit.

Question

The 2014 musical "Beautiful"
was based on the life
of what woman?

Answer

Carole King

2
POINTS

Question

What musical was the first to feature an all-female creative team?

Answer

Waitress

BONUS
Round!

(Give my regards to ...)

BONUS Round!

UP TO

7
POINTS

Can you sing with all the colors of the wind? Read aloud each color and show title below. Opposing team players must name the song title from that show that contains that specific color. (1 point for each correct answer for a maximum of 7 points.)

1 Green, *The Wedding Singer*
Answer: "All About the Green"

2 Red, *Porgy and Bess*
Answer: "A Red Headed Woman"

3 Black, *Les Misérables*
Answer: "Red and Black"

4 White, *The Secret Garden*
Answer: "A Fine White Horse"

5 Blue, *The Pirates of Penzance*
Answer: "How Beautifully Blue The Sky"

6 Purple, *Spring Awakening*
Answer: "The Song of Purple Summer"

7 Green, *School of Rock: The Musical*
Answer: "Horace Green Alma Mater"

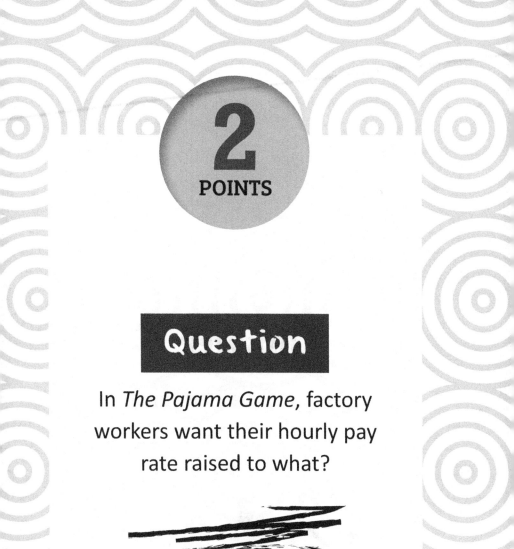

2
POINTS

Question

In *The Pajama Game*, factory workers want their hourly pay rate raised to what?

Answer

Seven-and-a-half cents

2 POINTS

Question

What song from *Gypsy* is widely considered to be one of the best 11 o'clock numbers of all time?

Answer

"Rose's Turn"

BONUS
Round!

(Be a showstopper!)

BONUS Round!

UP TO

7
POINTS

Belt it out! Read aloud each color and show title below.
Opposing team players must name the song title from that show
that contains that specific color.
(1 point for each correct answer for a maximum of 7 points.)

1 White, *The Music Man*
Answer: "My White Knight"

2 Yellow, *Motown The Musical*
Answer: "Itsy Bitsy Teeny Weeny Yellow Polka Dot Bikini"

3 Black, *Ain't Misbehavin'*
Answer: "Black and Blue"

4 Blue, *The Pajama Game*
Answer: "A New Town Is a Blue Town"

5 Green, *Sweeney Todd*
Answer: "Green Finch and Linnet Bird"

6 Brown, *Ragtime*
Answer: "Sarah Brown Eyes"

7 White, *Hair*
Answer: "White Boys"

2 POINTS

Question

What baseball team is featured in *Damn Yankees*?

Answer

Washington Senators

2 POINTS

Question

In what show did
Ricky Martin make his
Broadway debut?

Answer

Les Misérables

2
POINTS

Question

What was the name of
Danny's gang in *Grease*?

Answer

The Thunderbirds

2 POINTS

Question

The song "Have Yourself a Merry Little Christmas" was introduced in what musical?

Answer

Meet Me in St. Louis

3
POINTS

Question

In what year were the first
Tony Awards?

Answer

1947

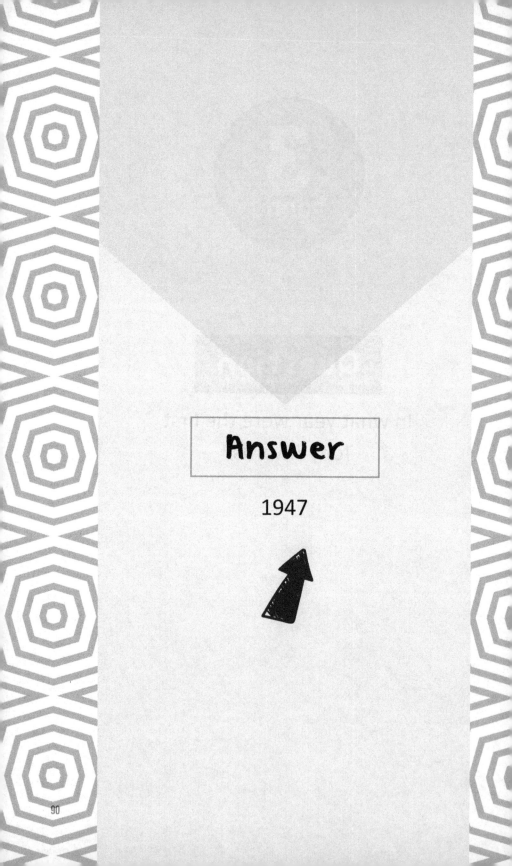

3
POINTS

Question

Who wrote the musical
Crazy for You?

Answer

George Gerswhin

BONUS

Round!

(The part you were born to play, baby.)

BONUS Round!

UP TO

12
POINTS

Set 1 minute on the clock. You will be asked to name as many songs as you can from one musical. No overtures, no entr'acte, no reprises, no orchestra-only songs. Your time begins after the name of the musical below is read aloud.
(1 point for each correct answer for a maximum of 12 points.)

The Sound of Music

"The Sound of Music"

"Morning Hymn/Alleluia"

"Maria"

"I Have Confidence"

"Sixteen Going on Seventeen"

"My Favorite Things"

"Climb Ev'ry Mountain"

"The Lonely Goatherd"

"Do-Re-Mi"

"Something Good"

"Edelweiss"

"So Long, Farewell"

1
POINT

Question

True or false: Through 2021, *Springsteen on Broadway* had the highest average ticket price in Broadway history with $405.89.

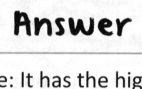

Answer

False: It has the highest average ticket price with $505.89!

1
POINT

Question

True or false: *Wicked* is the second highest-grossing musical of all time.

Answer

True! It has made
more than $1.2 billion.

3
POINTS

Question

What composer wrote *Jesus Christ Superstar*?

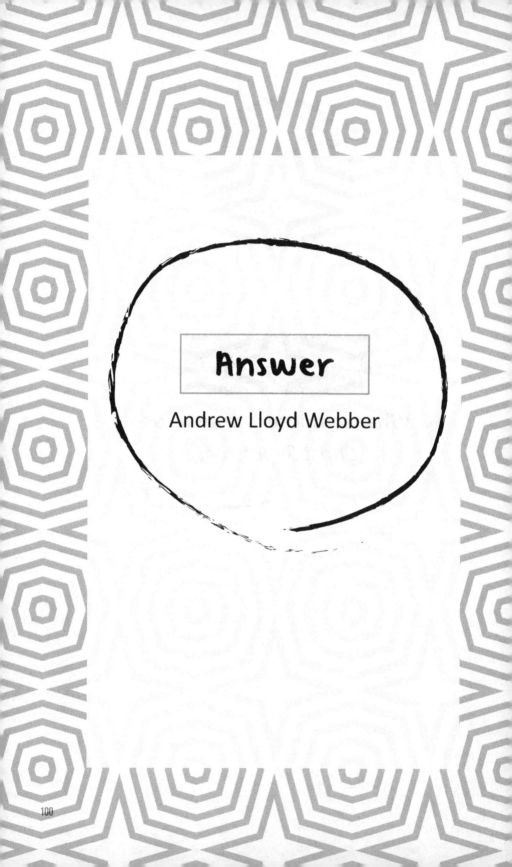

Answer

Andrew Lloyd Webber

Question

What composer wrote
Kiss Me, Kate?

Answer

Cole Porter

BONUS
Round!

(Your time to shine!)

BONUS Round!

UP TO

12
POINTS

Set 1 minute on the clock. You will be asked to name as many songs as you can from one musical. No overtures, no entr'acte, no reprises, no orchestra-only songs. Your time begins after the name of the musical below is read aloud.
(1 point for each correct answer for a maximum of 12 points.)

West Side Story

"Jet Song"

"Something's Coming"

"Maria"

"Tonight"

"America"

"Cool"

"One Hand, One Heart"

"Tonight (Quintet)"

"I Feel Pretty"

"Somewhere"

"Gee, Officer Krupke"

"A Boy Like That / I Have a Love"

2

POINTS

Question

Who made her
Broadway debut as Shug
Avery in 2015 in a revival
of *The Color Purple*?

Answer

Jennifer Hudson

2 POINTS

Question

According to King Charles in *Pippin*, war is what?

Answer

A science

2 POINTS

Question

Which play won
Best Musical at the Tony
Awards for 2021-22 season?

Answer

A Strange Loop

2 POINTS

Question

Trey Parker won three Tony
Awards for what musical?

Answer

The Book of Mormon

BONUS
Round!

(The curtain's going up.)

BONUS Round!

UP TO

5 POINTS

Who am I?

The four statements below apply to one specific Broadway character. You may take one guess after each statement is read.

Correct guess after one statement: 5 points
Correct guess after two statements: 4 points
Correct guess after three statements: 3 points
Correct guess after four statements: 2 points

Statement 1: I am a teenager.
Statement 2: I am a good dancer.
Statement 3: I'm a villain in my musical.
Statement 4: My mother was once Miss Baltimore Crabs.

ANSWER: Amber Von Tussle (*Hairspray*)

2 POINTS

Question

In the musical *School of Rock*, which musical instrument does the teacher Dewey Finn play?

Answer

Guitar

2

POINTS

Question

What musical features the song "We're in the Money"?

Answer

42nd Street

BONUS
Round!

(Now or never!)

BONUS Round!

UP TO

5
POINTS

Who am I?

The four statements below apply to one specific Broadway character. You may take one guess after each statement is read.

Correct guess after one statement: 5 points
Correct guess after two statements: 4 points
Correct guess after three statements: 3 points
Correct guess after four statements: 2 points

Statement 1: I am an aspiring actress.
Statement 2: I have a husband who loves me so.
Statement 3: I'm on trial for murder.
Statement 4: My name is going to be on everyone's lips.

ANSWER: Roxie Hart (*Chicago*)

2
POINTS

Question

What musical was the first to focus on the subject of teens and social media?

Answer

Dear Evan Hanson

2

POINTS

Question

Which Broadway musical
featured the first ever
nude scene?

Answer

Hair

BONUS
Round!

(Get ready to take a bow.)

BONUS Round!

UP TO

4

POINTS

Winter, spring, summer and fall ... Read aloud each season and show title below. Opposing team players must name the song title from that show that contains that specific season.
Sing your heart out!
(1 point for each correct answer for a maximum of 4 points.)

1 Spring, *South Pacific*
Answer: Younger Than Springtime

2 Summer, *Grease*
Answer: Summer Nights

3 Winter, *Matilda*
Answer: Love Me in the Winter

4 Fall, *Les Misérables*
Answer: A Little Fall of Rain

2 POINTS

Question

What character sings "Home"
in The Wiz?

Answer

Dorothy

2 POINTS

Question

What Broadway song was a No. 1 hit for Louis Armstrong in 1964?

Answer

"Hello, Dolly!"

BONUS
Round!

(Step into the spotlight.)

BONUS Round!

UP TO

4
POINTS

Are you playing with a full deck? Read aloud each card suit and show title below. Opposing team players must name the song title from that show that contains that specific card suit. Sing if you can!
(1 point for each correct answer for a maximum of 4 points.)

1 Spade, *Hair*
Answer: "Colored Spade"

2 Heart, *West Side Story*
Answer: "One Hand, One Heart"

3 Club, *Ain't Misbehavin'*
Answer: "Yacht Club Swing"

4 Diamond, *Aladdin*
Answer: "Diamond in the Rough"

Question

Which actress played
Fanny Brice when the musical
Funny Girl debuted in 1964?

Answer

Barbra Streisand

2 POINTS

Question

What year did *Cats* premiere?

Answer

1982

Question

Why does Tevye disown Chava
in *Fiddler on the Roof*?

Answer

She marries outside
the Jewish faith.

2 POINTS

Question

What is the name of the nightclub where Sally Bowles performs in *Cabaret*?

Answer

Kit Kat Klub

BONUS
Round!

(If you can make it here, you can make it anywhere.)

BONUS Round!

UP TO

5
POINTS

Read each show title and character name aloud.
The opposing team must name the character's
partner/romantic interest in the play.
(1 point for each correct answer for a maximum of 5 points.)

1 *Oklahoma*, Curly
Answer: Laurie

2 *Les Misérables*, Cosette
Answer: Marius

3 *Rent*, Angel
Answer: Collins

4 *Hamilton*, Alexander
Answer: Eliza

5 *Evita*, Eva
Answer: Juan

2 POINTS

Question

What was the name
of Annie's dog in *Annie*?

Answer

Sandy

2
POINTS

Question

What musical tells the story
of Elphaba and Galinda?

Answer

Wicked

BONUS
Round!

(Play with the excitement of Opening Night!)

BONUS Round!

UP TO

5
POINTS

Read each show title and character name aloud.
The opposing team must name the character's
partner/romantic interest in the play.
(1 point for each correct answer for a maximum of 5 points.)

1 *Rent*, Maureen
Answer: Joanne

2 *The Lion King*, Simba
Answer: Nala

3 *Waitress*, Dawn
Answer: Ogie

4 *Sunset Boulevard*, Norma
Answer: Joe

5 *Ellen*, Miss Saigon
Answer: Chris

Question

What musical is based on the play *Pygmalion* by George Bernard Shaw?

Answer

My Fair Lady

2 POINTS

Question

Who wrote the music
for *Billy Elliott: The Musical*?

Answer

Elton John

POINTS

Question

What is the first and last name of the main teen character in *Hairspray*?

Answer

Tracy Turnblad

POINTS

Question

Which musical features a group of drama students at New York's High School for the Performing Arts?

Answer

Fame

Question

What dancer injures his knee in *A Chorus Line*?

Answer

Paul

2

POINTS

Question

The cast of *Rent* taught us the number of minutes in one year. What is the number?

Answer

525,600

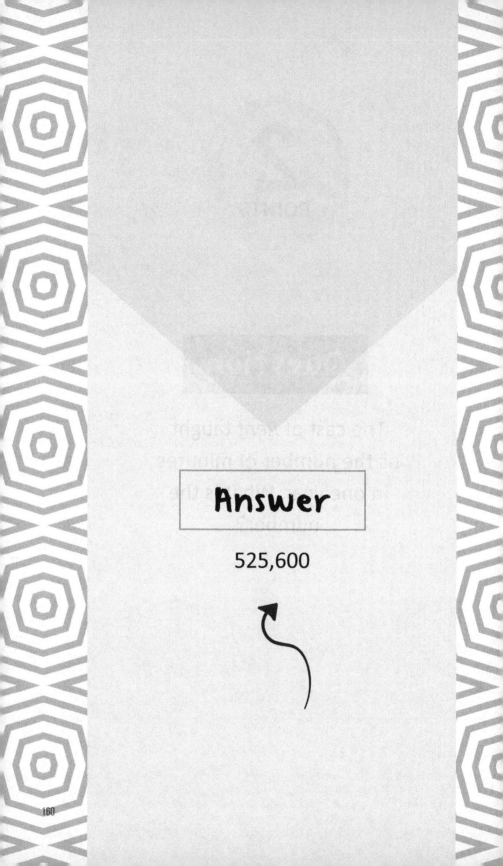

Question

True or false: It took creators 20,000 hours to make all of the puppets used in the musical *The Lion King*?

Answer

False. It took 37,000 hours!

1
POINT

Question

True or false: Julie Andrews made her Broadway debut in *The Sound of Music*.

Answer

False. She made her debut in
The Boy Friend in 1954.

BONUS
Round!

(All the world's a stage.)

BONUS Round!

UP TO

6
POINTS

One at a time, read aloud each show and song title
without saying the missing word.
Players on the opposing team must fill in the missing word.
(One point for each correct answer for a maximum of 6 points.)

1 *Six:* "Don't Lose Your _____"
Answer: Head

2 *Show Boat:* "Life Upon the _____ Stage"
Answer: Wicked

3 *A Strange Loop:* "Exile in _____"
Answer: Gayville

4 *Kiss Me Kate:* "I've Come to Wive It Wealthily in _____"
Answer: Padua

5 *In The Heights:* "Hundreds of _____"
Answer: Stories

6 *Aida:* "Fortune Favors the _____"
Answer: Brave

3
POINTS

Question

What was the first show to
open after a long COVID-19
Broadway shutdown?

Answer

Springsteen on Broadway
(June 26, 2021)

3
POINTS

Question

Which musical with an all-black cast broke the record for most Broadway performances in 1921?

Answer

Shuffle Along

BONUS
Round!

(Performance of a lifetime!)

BONUS Round!

UP TO

6 POINTS

One at a time, read aloud each show and song title
without saying the missing word.
Players on the opposing team must fill in the missing word.
(One point for each correct answer for a maximum of 6 points.)

1 *Ain't Misbehavin':* "When the _____ Bloom Again"
Answer: Nylons

2 *South Pacific:* "A Cockeyed _____"
Answer: Optimist

3 *Into the Woods:* "Careful My _____"
Answer: Toe

4 *The Secret Garden:* "A Bit of _____"
Answer: Earth

5 *Tommy:* "The Acid _____"
Answer: Queen

6 *The 25th Annual Putnam County Spelling Bee:*
"My Friend, The _____"
Answer: Dictionary

2
POINTS

Question

Which character in *Hamilton* sings "The Room Where It Happens"?

Answer

Aaron Burr

2
POINTS

Question

Which Broadway musical is based on the 1924 trials of accused murderers Beulah Annan and Belva Gaertner?

Answer

Chicago

3 POINTS

Question

What composer has won the
most Tony Awards?

Answer

Stephen Sondheim (8)

3 POINTS

Question

Who was the first person
to win six Tony Awards
for acting?

Answer

Audra McDonald

2
POINTS

Broadway seat rows are usually labeled using letters of the alphabet. But what letter is commonly skipped?

Answer

The letter I
(Too many people thought it
was row number 1.)

2 POINTS

Question

How many seats does a theater need to be considered "Broadway" instead of "Off-Broadway"?

Answer

500 seats minimum

BONUS
Round!

(A star is born.)

BONUS Round!

UP TO

5
POINTS

Who am I?

The four statements below apply to one specific Broadway character. You may take one guess after each statement is read.

Correct guess after one statement: 5 points
Correct guess after two statements: 4 points
Correct guess after three statements: 3 points
Correct guess after four statements: 2 points

Statement 1: All the girls love me.
Statement 2: I'm a pop star.
Statement 3: I was drafted by the Army.
Statement 4: I performed "One Last Kiss" on *The Ed Sullivan Show*.

ANSWER: Conrad Birdie (*Bye Bye Birdie*)

2 POINTS

Question

In the musical *Matilda*, what is Matilda's best friend's name?

Answer

Lavender

2
POINTS

Question

What musical featured a song called "Springtime for Hitler"?

Answer

The Producers

BONUS
Round!

(The big finale!)

BONUS Round!

UP TO

5 POINTS

Who am I?

The four statements below apply to one specific Broadway character. You may take one guess after each statement is read.

Correct guess after one statement: 5 points
Correct guess after two statements: 4 points
Correct guess after three statements: 3 points
Correct guess after four statements: 2 points

Statement 1: I'm a princess.
Statement 2: My play is based on a fairy tale.
Statement 3: I can't sleep.
Statement 4: My big number is "Shy."

ANSWER: Princess Winnifred
(*Once Upon a Mattress*)

2
POINTS

What was the first Disney
show to open on Broadway?

Answer

Beauty and the Beast (1994)

Question

What word is used to describe a theater that has no shows scheduled on a given day?

Answer

Dark

2 POINTS

Question

Cats was based on the work of what famous poet?

Answer

T.S. Eliot

2
POINTS

Question

Explain the significance
of 24601.

Answer

It's Jean Valjean's prison number in *Les Misérables*.

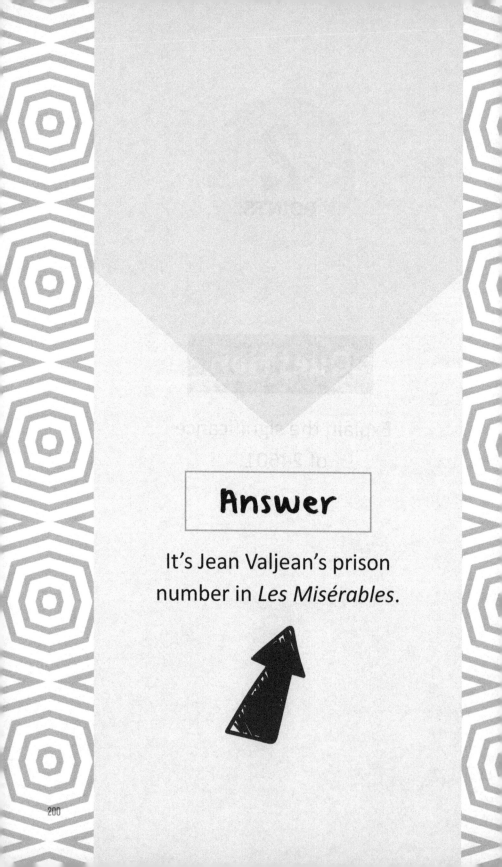

2
POINTS

Question

What Stephen King novel
was turned into a Broadway
musical that closed after just
16 previews and five regular
performances?

Answer

Carrie

2 POINTS

Question

After Sutton Foster won a Tony Award for *Thoroughly Modern Millie* in 2002, what piece of furniture did she buy?

Answer

A couch

Made in United States
Orlando, FL
27 December 2024

56606053R00114